2月 23日 97

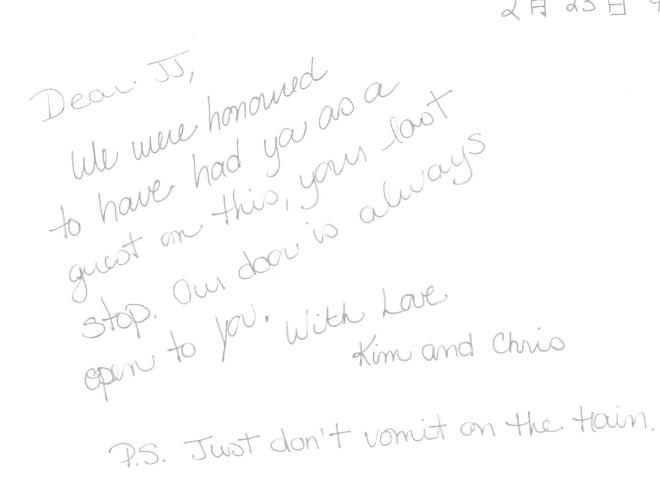

Dear JJ,

We were honoured to have had you as a guest on this, your last stop. Our door is always open to you. With Love

Kim and Chris

P.S. Just don't vomit on the train.

Illustrations credits:

**Archivio White Star/Marcello Bertinetti:**
Cover, back cover, 2-3, 10-11, 19, 23, 24, 28, 29, 30, 31, 34, 37, 38, 42-43, 46, 47, 48, 52, 53, 54, 55, 56, 58, 59, 60-61, 64, 68, 70, 86 top, 89, 94,-95, 96.

**Archivio White Star/Carlo De Fabianis:**
4, 6, 16 right, 22, 25, 32, 33, 39, 41, 44, 45, 51, 63, 69, 72, 75, 76, 85, 87, 88, 92-93.

**Archivio White Star/Angela White:**
1, 8, 9, 17, 18, 26, 27, 35, 36, 40-41, 49, 50, 62, 65, 66-67, 73, 74, 77, 78, 84, 86 bottom, 90, 91.

**Apa Photo Agency:**
57, 71.

**Dallas & John Heaton/Apa Photo Agency:**
7, 12-13, 14-15.

**R. Dorell/Apa Photo Agency:**
20.

**Allen F. Grazer/Apa Photo Agency:**
83.

**Tony Martorano/Apa Photo Agency:**
82.

**Maurizio Leigheb/Focus Team:**
79

**Paul Van Riel/Apa Photo Agency:**
21, 80-81.

**Nik Wheeler/Apa Photo Agency:**
16 left.

Translated by:
**Patricia Borlenghi**

Edited by:
**Heather Thomas**

© 1991 White Star
Via C. Sassone 24, Vercelli, Italy.

Printed and bound in Singapore.

First published in English in 1991 by Tiger Books International PLC, London.
ISBN 1-85501-171-9

# INSIDE
# TOKYO

TEXT
SIMONETTA CRESCIMBENE

DESIGN
PATRIZIA BALOCCO

TIGER BOOKS INTERNATIONAL

A resident of Tokyo is often described as an Edokko, although a genuine Edokko is someone whose family has lived there for at least three generations. Literally translated, it means 'son of Edo', thereby reinforcing the unshakable relationship between past and present which is the real force behind the modern and economically booming Tokyo of today. Edo, meaning 'at the mouth of the river', derives its name from its location on the Kanto plain near the Sumido estuary. The village of Edo sprung up around a castle built by a shogun beside the estuary in 1457 and it was not until 1868 that it became Japan's capital city and centre of government and its name was changed to Tokyo, meaning 'capital of the Orient'.

Tokyo's geographical location in the centre of Japan on Honshu, the largest and most populated of the Japanese islands, guarantees its supremacy. It straddles a well protected bay, and its enormously busy port has access to the Pacific Ocean. Its suburbs are spreading rapidly and inexorably into the fertile and intensively cultivated Kanto plain. Fortunately the march of progress has not totally spoilt the spectacular natural beauty of the surrounding countryside, and the distinctive conical shape of Mount Fuji still provides a magnificent backdrop to the city and is a potent symbol of the quintessential Japan.

Nature still has a geological hold over this land where volcanic eruptions and earthquakes have been frequent occurrences in Tokyo's chequered history. The great Kanto Earthquake and subsequent firestorm of 1923 devastated the city; over 91,000 people were killed and one-quarter of Tokyo's houses were destroyed. The high incidence of earthquakes and fires, or 'flowers of Edo' as they were sometimes poetically called, finally convinced Tokyo's planners that they should change from building in wood to stronger structures in concrete and stone.

Little of ancient Edo has survived, and the original districts of the city, divided by hills and woodland with little bridges suspended over streams and pagoda-roofed wooden temples are now just part of history. Only a handful of Shinto shrines, Buddhist temples and pagodas now remain. The 1923 Earthquake ushered in a new era with the almost total reconstruction of the city. Japanese initiative was tested once again in 1945 after the prolonged American bombardment of Tokyo. Now it is a bustling modern city with its foundations firmly rooted in rapid economic and industrial growth, yet adapting the philosophy of its forefathers to the new rhythms of twentieth-century city life. It has succeeded in creating an acceptable balance between overcrowded city suburbs and the traditional values of old Japan.

In spite of its Western-style office blocks and futuristic architecture, Tokyo is still first and foremost a city of the Orient. Although it has a great capacity to assimilate foreign cultures and indeed to exaggerate them, it still has the power to baffle Western visitors, especially Europeans.

In the city centre, the buildings are getting progressively higher, forever challenging the precarious geological nature of the land, as is demonstrated by the realisation of daring projects such as 'Sunshine 60' with its sixty floors. But turn the corner of a street and you may be transported back into the old Tokyo with its ascetically simple shrines and green gardens. The new skyscrapers provide a stark backdrop to the crowded streets

14-15 Even Japanese children wear religious costumes at some religious ceremonies and festivals. Real kimonos are incredibly expensive, costing thousands of US dollars, so many women opt for antique silk ones instead which cost a fraction of the price, or for a yukata, a modern version made of cotton.

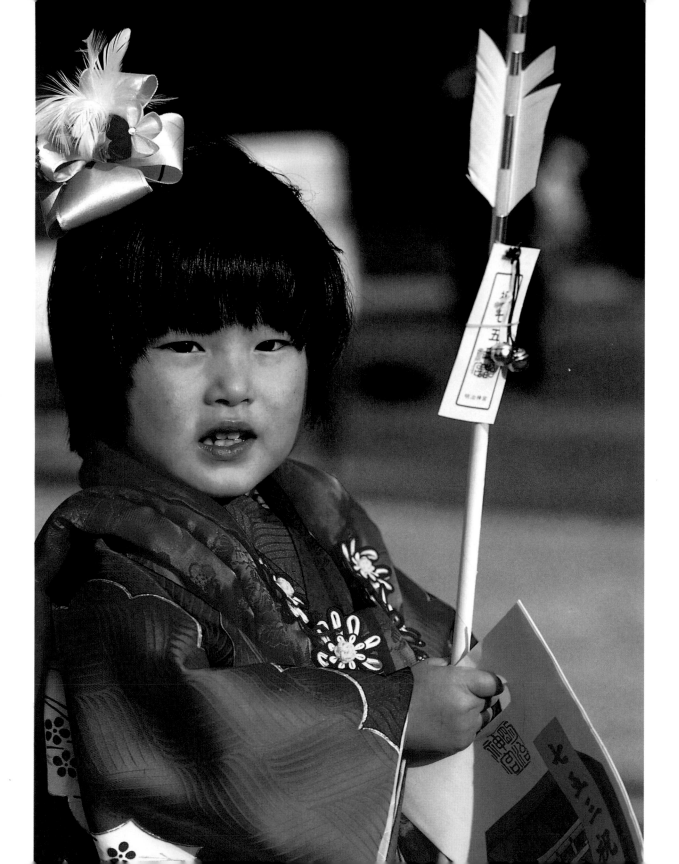

16 Educational standards in Japan are among the highest in the world, and state and private schools compete with one another to attract pupils. They often use the media for recruitment purposes, even advertising on television.

*17 The selection procedures are extremely rigorous and aspiring students must sit stressful and difficult entrance examinations. The parents of successful applicants may often have to pay extremely high fees depending on the schools' prestige and academic reputation.*

18 In recent years the number of girls applying to be geishas has declined as few are now willing to undertake the onerous ceremonial training. Geishas are still to be found in many of Tokyo's exclusive nightspots where businessmen are prepared to pay a high price for their services.

19 Japanese women have made great progress in recent years but they still live in a predominantly male-dominated society. Many women suffer discrimination in employment and assume a submissive and subordinate role in public. Many Japanese men still do not consider women to be their equals and do not respect them in business.

The traditional Japanese apartment, although often small and lacking space, is still the woman's undisputed realm and she is responsible for the children's upbringing and education.

21 Although conditions for women have improved significantly, Japan is still a sexist society, and real equality with men is still a long-term goal for many feminists. This is demonstrated by the fact that arranged marriages still account for one-third of the total, and that many companies expect their women employees to resign from their jobs on marriage or the birth of their first child.

22-23 The continuity between past and present and the equilibrium between tradition and innovation provide the stability and foundation for Japan's rapid economic growth and industrialization. In a relatively short period of time, Japan has been transformed from a military authoritarian society to a modern industrial state with a booming economy and an important role to play in international affairs, particularly in the Pacific.

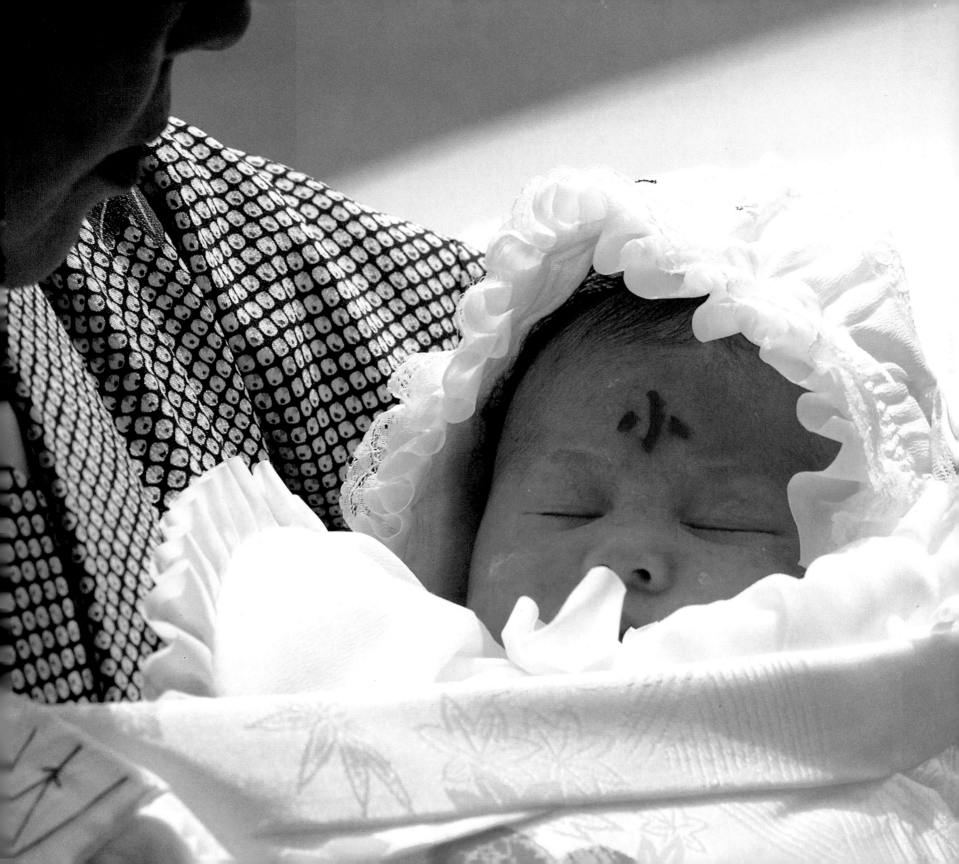

24 Travelling by subway in the rush hour can be an ordeal even for the most seasoned traveller. Often packed in tightly like sardines, commuters are physically pushed into the carriages at the busiest stations by the shirioshi in order that the automatic doors may be closed behind them.

25 The Shinkansen is the vanguard of Japan's superior and efficient transportation system. This so-called 'bullet train' can reach speeds of 175 miles per hour. One of the fastest trains in the world, it links Tokyo with the major cities in the north and south. Although expensive, it is a fast, efficient and comfortable way to explore Japan.

*26-27 Tokyo's roads are among the most congested in the world, and motor cycles are a popular way of weaving through traffic jams. In spite of the frustration of many motorists, traffic laws are universally respected and there are surprisingly few accidents.*

*28-29 Crowds of people throng the night-time streets of Ginza, Tokyo's premier entertainment district. The mass of neon signs burst into light with the onset of darkness transforming the area into the centre of the city's nightlife. Clubs, bars, discotheques and restaurants offering an infinite variety of entertainment and international cuisines vie with each other for customers.*

*G*inza is a tourist's paradise and renowned throughout the world for its acclaimed shopping malls. It derives its name from the old silver mint that stood on this site until 1800. Now it is a huge international shopping centre where you can buy almost anything and everything. Its fame has spread throughout the world and it easily rivals Fifth Avenue, the Faubourg St Honoré, Bond Street and the Via Veneto. The streets are lined with exclusive department stores and chic boutiques, and Tokyoites flock here after work and on Sundays to devote their leisure time to shopping – rather than resting!

Fashion and personal appearance are a national obsession for the Japanese and the last decade has seen an upsurge in Japanese designers like Kenzo, Issey Miyake and Yohji Yamamoto, who are now as well-known in the West as in their own country. Here, on the streets of Ginza, women in traditional heavy silk kimonos rub shoulders with others dressed in the latest fashions from the couturier houses of Paris and Milan.

At night the whole area is illuminated with flashing, multi-coloured neon signs inviting you to sample the hospitality of Ginza's many bars, restaurants, theatres and cabarets which offer a wide range of entertainment and amusements. Among the most typically Japanese are the *machiai* which are frequented by the last of the geishas. These women are regarded by the Japanese as the embodiment of feminine accomplishments. They are graceful dancers and singers and entertain businessmen and powerful executives who can afford to pay for their services. They wear traditional dress and classic white make-up and undergo a formidable training to learn their well-practised arts.

36-37 Tokyo's Disneyland is a popular venue for both adults and children who crowd into the huge entertainment complex from 7.30am to 10.30pm every day. Since 1983 it has opened its doors to over 10,000,000 visitors every year. As in its American counterparts, children are enthralled by Mickey-san and all the other familiar Disney characters. Regular shuttle buses operate at frequent intervals throughout the day between Disneyland and Tokyo Station. The enterprise has proved that the Disney characters have universal appeal to fire children's imaginations.

38  This photograph is testament to the geometric harmony of the Tokyo Tower – Japan's answer to the Eiffel Tower in Paris. An imposing structure of 1089 feet, the Tokyo Tower was built in 1958 and came to symbolize the spirit of reconstruction after World War II. Every year it attracts millions of visitors who admire the panoramic views of the city from its viewing platforms. On a clear day you may even see snow-capped Mount Fuji in the distance. The tower is also home to an aquarium and a waxworks, the first in Asia.

39 The New York 'love hotel' surmounted by a huge replica of the Statue of Liberty offers its clients the opportunity to hire rooms on an hourly basis. Surprisingly, many are married couples.

40 The skyline of the affluent Shinjuku district in the western part of Tokyo has changed in recent years with the construction of several soaring and distinctive skyscrapers. Shinjuku holds the record for the highest property values in the city. Here also are the bars, cinemas, theatres, jazz clubs and nightspots of Kabukicho, one of Tokyo's most popular entertainment districts.

41 Here in the heart of Ginza, like the rest of Tokyo, space is very precious and the crowded urban skyline casts shadows across the streets below. Few home-owners can afford to live in the inner-city suburbs and most commute to their Tokyo offices by train. Development is continuous and buildings are torn down and rebuilt. Countless new shopping centres, office blocks and condominiums spring up all over the city.

42-43 Driving in Tokyo is challenging for the Western visitor as the roads are rarely as light in traffic as shown overleaf and most signs are in Japanese only with the exception of the major routes which are numbered in Roman script. Most city streets and flyovers are congested with traffic throughout the day. There are frequent traffic lights and illegally parked cars which slow down the traffic flow. In fact, illegal parking is such a problem that over 60,000 cars are towed away to pounds every day to be reclaimed later by their rightful owners.

44-45 *Akihabara is heaven on earth for electronics and computer buffs who crowd its narrow streets looking for the latest electronic wizardry and gadgets. This district of Tokyo is world famous for selling the latest models in Japanese innovative electronic technology. Prices are often heavily discounted and purchasers are expected to haggle to get further reductions.*

*46 In the centre of Tokyo you can play golf in the most unlikely places. This is a roof-top driving range where devotees tee off enthusiastically, high above the bustling city streets. Golf is fast becoming a Japanese national obsession, but there is so little available land for building new courses around Tokyo that many people practise religiously at inner-city clubs and driving ranges.*

*47 Pachinko is a form of pinball which is exclusive to Japan. It is increasingly popular with young and old alike, and Tokyo has hundreds of these pinball arcades, all crowded with people, playing the machines.*

*I*n the busy streets of Tsukiji, which is the link between the city and the ocean, is the biggest fish market in the world with over 400 species of fish on sale. Fish is still the main staple of Japanese cooking and is highly prized for its freshness and flavour, especially in *sushi*. There are no romantic views to be enjoyed walking along the seafront here. The docks have been carved up by the railway lines which lead to Yokohama, the only remaining part of the Minato district which has lost all its original identity by its development into a prestigious residential and diplomatic area. Here, the British, United States and French embassies can be found alongside some of the city's most elegant addresses.

Not far away is Roppongi which takes its name from six feudal shoguns with arboreal names who once lived there. Today, the district's chaotic roads network is dominated by the gigantic Tokyo Tower. Modelled on the Eiffel Tower in Paris, it is 100 feet taller and offers breathtaking panoramic views of the whole city from its crow's nest viewing platform.

The intellectually aspiring visitor can be certain of finding interesting places to visit in Kanda. Visit the Kanda Myojin Shrine, rebuilt in 1934 to reproduce faithfully the original with its cherry tree-lined courtyard guarded by statues of dogs and dragons. A short walk away, in the streets of Jimbocho, are bookstores galore with antiquarian booksellers rubbing shoulders with second-hand bookstores, wholesalers and publishers. Here you can browse side by side with students and elderly gentlemen making notes, enjoying a good read or examining a rare edition.

Kanda is a paradise for anyone interested in woodblock-printed antiquarian books, paperbacks, including Western ones, and old

49 Shopping is a typical Sunday pastime and viewed by the Japanese as a form of relaxation. Department stores, shops and boutiques all open on public holidays so that people in full-time employment can shop on their days off. Japanese women are enthusiastic shoppers and Tokyo offers a wide range of consumer products to meet every individual's needs.

prints. All over Tokyo you will see people reading in the most unlikely places – standing at dawn in the congested subway carriages, or in the evenings seated on benches in the city parks and peaceful gardens.

The standard of education in Japan is uniformly high and the educational system is one of the best in the world. From the earliest stage, it emphasises the concept of competitiveness at work. Students need good examination results and qualifications to gain entry to the private, state and municipal universities, and competition is fierce. This selection process divides secondary/high schools into prestigious superior institutions and those that provide a more elementary standard education. This educational hierarchy forces thousands of aspiring students and their families into undergoing a continuous cycle of entrance exams and interviews which are costly in terms of effort and expense. It is the dream of every student to attend one of the faculties in the respected University of Tokyo, which is located in the cultural centre of Bunkyo-ku. In these austere buildings, generations of future brilliant scientists, technologists, entrepreneurs and other members of Japan's professional élite who have been responsible for creating the prosperity of modern-day Tokyo have been educated. The city's healthy economy and commercial success are due to the skills and entrepreneurial spirit of these people, together with their natural propensity for order, discipline and courtesy which characterize Japanese society and business.

The relationship between a company and its employees is based on reciprocal loyalty, whether in an office or on a factory assembly line. Posters encourage mutual respect and a sense of

comradeship within corporate organizations. Offices and factories open punctually and often the first 30 minutes of the working day are devoted to exercise which relaxes the employees' bodies and minds in preparation for the long working day ahead. After work, many Tokyo office workers accompany their colleagues to Ginza or another fashionable area where they can enjoy a glass of sake in the bars and nightclubs. After a few glasses of this traditional Japanese drink, their habitual formality of manner gradually disappears. In the summer rooftop beer gardens, they sometimes dance or even watch sumo wrestling. Women rarely participate in these 'men-only' outings but it is not unusual for companies to arrange special singles parties for their unmarried employees. Tokyo offers a wide range of activities, leisure pursuits and entertainments so there is always something for the single person to do. Public bathhouses used to be very popular in the city and some still remain in the older neighbourhoods providing a meeting-place for the locals who relax in the steaming hot water after a day's work. However, they are gradually being replaced by modern Western-style saunas.

Golf and archery are the great sporting passions of many Tokyoites. In many inner-city golf clubs and driving ranges you can watch hundreds of people firing arrows at nearby targets as you tee off! There are many stadium-sized multi-level driving ranges where enthusiastic and dedicated Japanese golfers practise their technique and golfing skills even into the night. Because of the shortage of land, membership fees for Tokyo's most exclusive golf clubs are incredibly high and not within the range of most people. However, the Japanese are so passionately committed to

*52 Shinjuku at night is an area of great contrasts – amusement arcades, sex parlours and seedy bars exist side by side with international hotels, smart restaurants and theatres. The streets and narrow alleyways of the Kabukicho district are lined with brightly coloured neon lights advertising strip-shows and nightclubs.*

golf that they think nothing of driving for several hours through heavy traffic at a weekend to get out of the city and play a round of golf on an overcrowded course in Tokyo's environs.

Bowling is another popular sport and there are more than 60 bowling alleys in the city. It is almost impossible to swim in the summer months when the public pools are saturated with thousands of visitors literally unable to move in the water. Even in the evenings, you may have to stand in line in the water and take turns at swimming a length, so popular is swimming with Tokyo's office workers. Sophisticated slides, inflatables and watersports compensate somewhat for the overcrowded conditions but as a general rule visitors are best advised to stick to their hotel pools. Lovers of mountain sports and skiing can experience similar problems, especially those who want to ski on the plastic slopes at Tokyo's Disneyland. But not all sports are so over-subscribed; for example, there are numerous Man-made ponds and lakes where, for a modest price, urban fishermen can lose themselves in the heart of the city. Every waterway and river bank becomes a meeting place for friends, and it is not unusual to see men with fishing lines seated elbow to elbow along the entire length of the moat surrounding the Imperial Palace Park!

Tokyo's residents have a stong sense of community, stronger than in most Western cities, which is particularly powerful and cohesive within each district of the city. In every neighbourhood, there is an active residents' association, and meetings and activities are well attended. In this city of small villages, people often have a fierce loyalty to their neighbourhood and take a pride in maintaining its standards and local identity. This helps compensate Tokyoites for

the loss of identity that can be experienced when living in such a sprawling, amorphous and bustling city. Visiting one's neighbours is a tradition reinforced by social customs and formalities – calling cards are left and gifts exchanged thereby fostering mutual understanding and friendship. The Japanese place great emphasis on social harmony, which they call *wa*, and this must be achieved and preserved in every level of society and in their everyday lives - in business, in politics, in leisure, at work, in the home and in friendships.

Throughout the year, every district has at least one *matsuri* festival. These temporarily transform the lives of the people and the appearance of the district. The locals wear colourful, traditional costumes and decorate the little altars and Shinto shrines with paper flowers. As the temple bells summon the faithful, they pay homage to the two principal professions of faith – Shintoism and Buddhism, especially Zen Buddhism.

*56-57 After work many businessmen and office workers spend the evening in the company of their colleagues in Tokyo's summer roof-top beer gardens. Many types of entertainment are on offer from dancing to female wrestling! Perhaps the most popular form of Tokyo nightlife is the uniquely Japanese karaoke bar where normally staid and restrained businessmen belt out songs into a microphone to recorded music, reading the words off a video screen or from a songbook. Many Western visitors feel awkward if called upon to perform in one of these bars, but your Japanese hosts may be offended if you refuse to sing. Most people sing out of tune so you should not worry unduly about singing in key!*

Asakusa is a popular suburb in northern Tokyo which has a traditional appeal for many Tokyoites and still radiates some of the atmosphere and culture of the old city. Here, you can still find buildings that have survived the earthquakes, fires and bombings, and indeed the area acts as a bridge linking the traditions of the past with those of the present. Crowds of people congregate here, especially at weekends, around the district's spiritual centre – the enormous Asakusa Kannon Temple. This ancient temple was founded in the seventh century and is dedicated to the Buddhist goddess Bodhisattva Kannon. Unfortunately the original temple was destroyed and the present reconstruction, although a faithful replica of its predecessor, was built in 1958. However, it does contain some of the original decorations and ancient artefacts and relics.

On public holidays, a visit to Asakusa is an unforgettable experience for the visitor to Tokyo, especially on New Year's Eve when the area is thronged with crowds of worshippers. Religious ceremonies and formalized dancing take place as twelve temple bells are struck at regular intervals throughout the night. On this special occasion, the Emperor himself, dressed in ceremonial costume, welcomes visitors with a prayer for New Year prosperity. Each year on the fifteenth day of June there is a comparable pilgrimage to the Shinto temple in Asakusa. On this festive occasion, both male and female priests dressed in traditional robes and bearing elaborately decorated ritualistic relics, walk in procession to the shrine.

58-59 Auctions start at 5am at Tsukiji Wholesale Fish Market – the largest in the world. A huge range of fish – over 400 varieties – are on display here, but the frozen tuna, which hails from the southern Pacific, is the most highly prized. A single carcase can sell for enormous sums to the wholesalers who then distribute the fish to Tokyo's many shops, sushi bars and restaurants.

60-61 The fruit and vegetable market in Kanda sells enormous quantities of fresh produce every day, with trading starting at day break. The Japanese insist on quality and freshness in all their food, and only the best and freshest fruit and vegetables are acceptable.

62 Tokyo lies at the heart of Japan's new industrial society. Here cars are manufactured on Nissan's assembly line; executives meet to direct and plan factory business; while in one of Tokyo's famous 'capsule' hotel rooms, a visiting businessman spends the night at minimal cost in minimal space. These men-only capsule hotels are also a popular choice for commuters staying overnight in the capital, and workers who miss the last train home.

63 The HSST is a revolutionary new train. Designed by Japan Airlines, it is propelled by electro-magnetic motors and can reach speeds of 350 miles per hour as it travels suspended over the rail tracks through the heart of Japan.

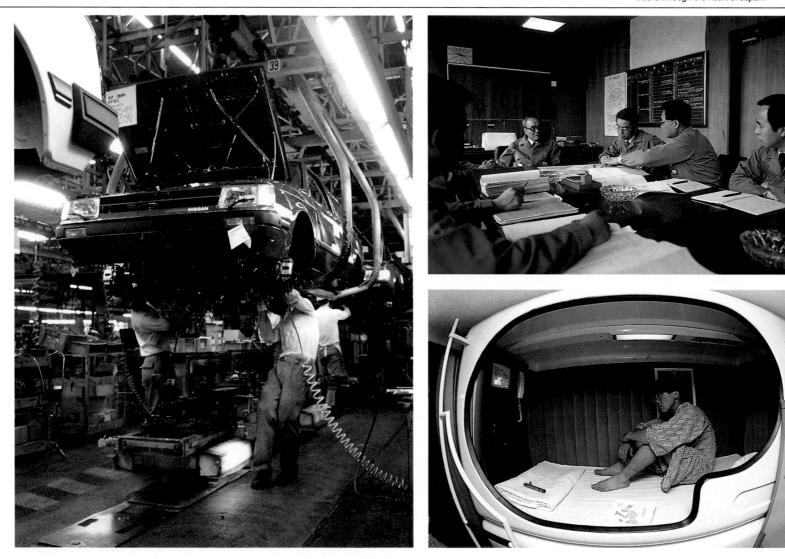

*64-65 Although this looks like an abstract modern sculpture, in reality this anechoic chamber is part of the Tsukuba Space Station and is used for measuring satellite radio frequencies. Opposite is one of the many technicians who work there.*

*66-67 The Tokyo Stock Exchange in Kabutocho is one of the most important financial markets in the world, and the dealing is fast and furious on the crowded floor. The area around the exchange is the commercial centre of Japan and home to the major banks and the headquarters of big corporations.*

68 Most of the visitors to the Japan Science Museum, situated in the Imperial Palace Gardens, are schoolchildren and parties of students.

69 The multi-level Tokyo Metropolitan Art Museum is situated in Ueno like many other city museums and galleries. Twice yearly the Museum exhibits its fine collection of contemporary Japanese works of art. It specializes in staging exhibitions by aspiring new painters and sculptors.

72 Ueno Park is a popular haunt for Tokyoites in
spring when the cherry blossom is in bloom. It is
also the home of Japan's most prestigious
museums, art galleries and concert halls as well as
the national zoo with its rare giant pandas.

73 In the congested city streets, traditional costumes are still worn with natural grace and ease by women of all ages. Whereas new silk kimonos are hideously expensive and are almost works of art, antique kimonos of equal beauty and quality can be purchased for a fraction of the price.

The crowd of spectators acclaim the pair of Yokozuna (grand champions) at a critical moment in a Sumo wrestling contest. This 2000-year-old sport is extremely popular with millions of enthusiasts who follow it on television and attend the tournaments. Each contestant attempts to force his opponent out of a circle 14 feet 10 inches in diameter, or to touch down with part of his body other than his feet. Tournaments, or basho, are held annually every January, May and September in Tokyo.